Power over Anxiety...

No Longer Overpowered

Deborah Pinkston, Ph.D. LPC

This book is dedicated to the individuals who

have sought relief from their anxiety-

Clients, family members, and friends.

May you glean strategies from these pages

to slow down the cycle of anxiety and

find peace.

Contact the author at:

Debbiepinkston59@gmail.com

Copyright © 2015

Cover Photo: William Oldham

Power over Anxiety...
No Longer Overpowered

Power over Anxiety…
No Longer Overpowered

1. Introduction

For some time I have intended to write a short, practical book about anxiety, but somehow never stopped long enough to write. My interest in writing this book stems from my own past experiences and struggles with anxiety and a panic disorder, from helping many counseling clients cope with anxiety, and helping family members and friends as they struggled with anxiety.

This book isn't written for the individual who occasionally experiences a little anxiety due to stress or life changes, but it is intended to serve those who suffer from crippling anxiety that has taken on a life of its own. In other words, here I'm not addressing the normal anxiety due to a specific circumstance. If this is your situation you may not need the techniques outlined in this book. The anxiety I'm addressing here is the kind that feeds itself, snowballing and getting worse over time, causing the one who suffers to live in a cycle of anxiety that looks something like this: "I was anxious about ... and I experienced a panic attack. Then I had another panic attack. Then I started having intense anxiety about the panic attacks. Then I had anxiety about having a problem with anxiety and feared having more panic attacks. Then I spent every waking moment trying to rid myself of the anxiety". On and on it goes and the anxiety itself is the problem, not a circumstance or situation.

I can honestly say to my clients that I know what it's like to wake up with a pounding heart, thoughts racing and feeling like I'm going crazy, because I have. It's now a distant memory, but the memory is based on one of the darkest times of my life.

My first bout with intense anxiety began in my senior year of High School. I remember sitting in the living room, looking through a magazine. I vaguely remember thinking that I would never look like the images of the beautiful women in the magazines and feeling a little sad...and then BOOM! Out of nowhere (or so I thought), my heart started to pound furiously, I started sweating profusely, my mind went blank, except for the most horrible, indescribable TERROR that I had every felt. My next thought was that I was going crazy. I was sure that I had lost my mind! It took me a while to calm down, but that was followed by a pervasive dread and fear that the horrible experience would happen again. I eventually overcame the anxiety and was well for several years.

My second bout with intense anxiety was in my early thirties. I was physically run down, emotionally exhausted from several difficult situations in my life, and again, "out of the blue" panic and anxiety set in. I recognized what I was feeling as the same thing I had experienced in high school, and frantically started applying all the techniques I could remember using back then. None of it seemed to work, except perhaps to keep me from "the edge". I struggled on my own for 1 ½ years, trying with all my might to figure this out and make it go away.

I finally got well, and today I'm anxiety-free most of the time, with an occasional flare up when I'm under extreme stress, but it's quickly dealt with and over. If you're reading this book, most likely you're all too familiar with the symptoms of anxiety, and you're desperately trying to find a way out of the maze. I hope that my personal experience, my studies and work with clients will be of help to you.

I encourage you to read one section of this book at a time and practice the skill or concept for a week or two before moving to the next chapter. It's helpful to keep a record of the concept you're working on as you work through this book, with the date, the skill or concept, the difficulty and challenges in carrying it out, and the outcome. Make a note of the changes you observe in the level and intensity of your anxiety.

"There's serenity on the other side of this" a dear friend once told me. She was right. My hope is that you too will find serenity.

2. The Power of Understanding Anxiety

When we understand the nature of anxiety, how it works, why we experience it, and how it perpetuates itself, we gain power over it. The lack of knowledge is a lack of power. Knowing what we're experiencing gives us the advantage.

Anytime we're faced with something new and frightening, not understanding what's happening is one of the most frightening aspects of the ordeal. When we're confronted with a physical illness, such as a herniated disk or cancer, the first thing physicians encourage us to do (a good physician) is to become informed and educated about our illness or condition. The more we understand something, the better equipped we are to tackle it. The same applies to anxiety.

One of the most frightening aspects of my anxiety in high school was that I had no clue what was going on in my brain and body. At that time (in the mid 70's) there was little available information about mental illness and I hadn't heard anyone speak of depression and anxiety in casual conversation.

I hadn't seen anything in books or magazines, and the internet didn't exist at that time. (Steve Jobs and his team were diligently working in their garage and first introduced personal computers in 1984). There was literally no source of information for me to understand what was happening to me. I was terrified!

I was so afraid of speaking up and being considered "crazy" that I kept my plight to myself. I didn't dare mention my craziness to my parents. What if they took me to a mental institution? Those thoughts only fueled my anxiety. It was a very lonely and fearful time. If I had spoken up I might have found a person who knew about depression and anxiety and who might have been able to guide me or inform me about treatment options. I urge you to speak up if you're suffering from anxiety!

When I went through my second episode of anxiety and panic I was in my early thirties. I went to the local library and checked out as many books as I could on the topic of anxiety and mental illness and I read for hours. Personal computers were on the market at the time and we owned one, but the internet was in its infancy. Through reading books, I learned about depression and anxiety, medications, treatment approaches and more. I learned more from my doctor and counselor, and from a friend who is a nurse. By the early 90's, depression and anxiety were talked about more openly.

Today mental illness is a topic that is talked about more openly than in previous years and there is a multitude of information on the internet. While we can't believe everything we read on the internet, there are some reliable websites (listed at the end of the book) and physicians are usually knowledgeable and open to speaking with their patients about mental illness. Most of us know someone who suffers from a mental illness, whether it's depression, anxiety, OCD, or bipolar depression. We're aware that many individuals around us and even within our own family have taken or are currently taking medication. The stigma is slowly falling away and we're more open now than ever to admit and discuss our struggles.

I encourage you to learn as much as you can about anxiety disorders. Look online, check out books, and yes, you're reading this book! Congratulations on taking the first step to getting well.

The Nature of Anxiety

As you probably already know, some anxiety is good. We need it to stay safe, to do our best, to strive for our family's wellbeing, and so on. A little test anxiety is good and leads us to study instead of slacking off before the exam. Some anxiety on the job is good and motivates us to do our best.

Our bodies have a built in alarm system, designed to alert us when we're in danger, and lead us to do something about it. This is what is referred to as the "fight or flight" response. Some have added "freeze" to the concept, so "fight, flight, or freeze" could be a needed response at times. If we realize at night that there's an intruder in our home, we might do one of three things: decide to get our baseball bat (or gun) and confront the intruder, which would constitute the "fight" response. We might gather our family and run out the back door, the "flight" response. Or, if you're like me, you might try to be as quiet as possible, lay still in bed, and hope to go unnoticed, the "freeze" response.

We often say we would do "this" or "that" in an emergency situation, but in all honesty, we don't really know how we'll react at the time. I once was robbed of my car at gunpoint while living in Venezuela, and as the robber was getting into the passenger seat of my car with a gun pointed at me, I opened my door and got out, running around to the other side of the car to get my friend's two small children to safety. I didn't think about it, I just ran! My "fight, flight or freeze" response kicked in and I ran to safety. A big "Thank you" to my body's natural response!

What happens in the case of an anxiety or panic disorder is that our body goes into this "alarm mode" when there's really no need for it. We're not being chased by a bear, we're not faced with an impending tragedy, and we're not being held at gunpoint, but for some reason our bodies feel as though we're in danger. BAM! Out of nowhere panic sets in, and we're sweating profusely, our heart feels like it's going to jump out of our chest, and we feel like running away. We feel dizzy and terrified. There's no danger but our bodies act as if something terrible is going to happen. In my case I thought I was going crazy and that my mind was totally messed up. That fueled more fear and anxiety, and the vicious cycle began!

Soon we're anxious about the anxiety, and it becomes a vicious cycle. What happened to our brain? How do we deal with it? How can we make it go away? How can we get our "old brain back"? We soon become obsessed with dealing with our anxiety, trying to find the cause and the cure. We look for physical illnesses that might cause the anxiety. Sometimes there are physical illnesses and conditions that can contribute to anxiety, such as PMS, thyroid problems, blood sugar issues, and others, but in most cases there is no physical ailment that can explain our anxiety. At this point, the anxiety has a life of its own, it seems. We spend every waking moment consumed with thoughts of the anxiety, trying to find a way out. We may seek out a doctor, psychiatrist, counselor, pastor, or healer who can explain what's happening and make us better. We want a cure, a formula, a switch we can flip that will make it all go away. We may spend hours reading our Bible and praying. We may look incessantly for clues as to how to make this monster go away. For me it felt as though I was a hamster running on a wheel, running faster and faster, trying harder and harder to stop the anxiety, but all my efforts only made it worse.

Hereditary Factors

Some mental illnesses run in families, and when I counsel individuals with anxiety or depression, I ask if anyone in their family has suffered from a mental illness. Sometimes they can identify a father, mother, sibling, aunt or uncle who dealt with anxiety or depression. The potential for experiencing an anxiety disorder is a reality for anyone, but more so for those with a family history of anxiety, just as heart problems are possible for anyone but more common for those with a family history of cardiovascular disease.

This leads us to our next point: Anxiety disorders, as well as depression and other mental illnesses, are physiological in nature. They may be triggered by stressful or traumatic events (or not) but they are physical in nature. They are not the result of "sin in your life" as some ultra-religious types might say. If that were the case, we could confess our sin and get over the anxiety. That certainly would be an easy fix! Upon the "guidance" of a well-meaning pastor, I confessed my sins over and over, those I could remember and those I thought I might have forgotten...but my anxiety continued. I wish it had been as easy as confessing my sins! My anguish only grew stronger and I thought perhaps I wasn't living the spiritual life I should be and I didn't feel God's closeness as I had previously.

The fact is that our brain is an organ, just like our kidneys, our heart, our liver, or our stomach. As an organ, it accomplishes certain functions, and in order to do its job well, it needs certain optimal conditions. For our thought processes to function smoothly, our brains produce neurotransmitters, which carry impulses from one neuron to the next. There are like minibuses that move the information on down the chain of neurons. In order to produce these neurotransmitters, certain nutrients are necessary. Without getting technical, I'll just share that our brain needs Vitamin D, either through sunshine or supplements. Our brain also needs the B vitamins, especially Vitamin B6. It needs Omega3, and certain minerals such as Magnesium and Zinc. Recent studies have shown that iodine is also necessary for optimal health and most of us do not get enough iodine in our diets. I recommend supplements of all of the above mentioned vitamins and minerals to my clients.

Serotonin is an important neurotransmitter which has everything to do with anxiety and depression. Serotonin acts as a natural tranquilizer when it's produced adequately. With good serotonin levels, we feel optimistic, energetic, motivated, we have a good appetite, we sleep well, and we feel that somehow we can face life's challenges with success. In the face of difficulties, we feel confident that we'll be able to overcome them. Our focus is outward, on life around us, and not inward. Those who suffer from anxiety tend to focus inwardly in an obsessive manner and this inward focus only compounds their anxiety. They feel that they're slaves to their brains.

When serotonin levels are lower than normal, along with other neurotransmitters and nutrients, our brains suffer, and we slowly, without realizing it lose our confidence that we can meet life's challenges with hope. Soon our problems loom larger than before, and we feel much smaller and unable to face the challenges. At that point, our primitive brain, the amygdala, sends out alarm signals and anxiety sets in.

But what contributes to these changes in neurotransmitters? In addition to a deficiency in the vitamins and minerals mentioned previously, other factors play a role. Chronic stress, accidents, illnesses, childbirth, surgery, major losses and many other life events can slowly wear down our brain's ability to stand firm in the face of life's challenges. In other words, when life sucks, instead of our brain rising to the challenge and kicking in more serotonin, noradrenaline, and gamma-aminobutyric acid (GABA) and other critical neurotransmitters, we actually become depleted of these precious, life-giving substances that make our brains tick well. Unfortunately it's when we most need our brains that our brains sometimes betray us.

Brain Structures Involved in Anxiety

I'm not a medical doctor, nor do I have extensive knowledge of how our brains work. What I have learned has been through reading and attending continuing education courses and conferences. A psychiatrist or neurologist would be much better equipped to discuss this topic, but I will share very general information that might help the layman understand how our brains function.

Certain brain structures play a significant role in anxiety and our body's ability to remain calm. The autonomic nervous system is comprised of the sympathetic nervous system and the parasympathetic nervous system. The sympathetic nervous system speeds up processes such as the heart rate, breathing, and tightens muscles when faced with stressful events. The parasympathetic nervous system does the opposite, helping the body to slow down the heart rate and relax the muscles. In other words, one works to get us ready to fight or run from threats, and the other helps us to return to a calm state. These two systems are supposed to work together to maintain the body's balance.

The amygdala, part of the sympathetic nervous system, is designed to keep us alive and is responsible for signaling danger and triggers the fear response. It sends signals throughout our body to prepare to fight or run away. When I had panic attacks, I had a strong urge to get up and run out of the room. The amygdala contacts the hypothalamus and stress chemicals are produced in several organs, such as adrenaline, norepinephrine and dopamine in the case of the sympathetic nervous system, which prepare us for physical action to remove the threat. Then the parasympathetic nervous system calls for the production of cortisol, endorphins, acetylcholine, oxytocin, and GABA to restore balance (Schore, 2001).

The hippocampus is also part of the limbic system and it helps to encode information. It stores memories of past painful experiences, and relates new events to past events. The insular cortex near the thalamus translates the experiences of our senses into emotions and the thoughts that we have about those emotions.

The right orbitofrontal cortex is part of the prefrontal cortex and is the most sophisticated part of the brain. It is located behind and above the eyes, basically behind our foreheads. It is very important in dealing with anxiety, because it helps to weigh the threat in a logical manner and helps to calm down the overreaction of the amygdala. In a sense, the orbitofrontal cortex helps to decode the signals sent by the amygdala and decide if a real threat exists (LeDoux, 1996).

Exciting research is being conducted to better understand the relationship of these brain structures to anxiety and how to promote self-calming methods to help those who suffer from anxiety.

The Role of our Thoughts

The way that we think can also influence our brain's chemistry, and recent studies have proven the relationship between our thoughts and our brain. It has been proven that our negative thinking, over time, erodes our brain chemistry, creates neural pathways that become more and more entrenched, and our ability to cope with life gradually slips away. Conversely, our deliberate, positive thoughts can improve our brain's function. In the next chapter we'll go into more depth about the power of our thoughts.

3. *The Power of Our Thoughts*

I mentioned earlier that when I experienced my first episode of anxiety in high school, I was looking at a magazine when panic hit me like a ton of bricks. Looking back, I remember thinking something like "I'll never be as pretty as these ladies in the magazine…I'll never have beautiful clothes like these…I'm a poor girl who probably won't get anywhere in life…etc". Without realizing it, over the previous few months I had let my once positive attitude go downhill. My boyfriend had cut off our relationship, I was leaving home for college soon, and life just sucked for me right then-or so I thought. Those negative thoughts slowly permeated my mindset and without realizing it I was setting myself up for a very frightening and unwelcome mental illness.

I struggled with the anxiety for several months, and then came across a book that a friend had in her apartment. She regularly let me borrow books, and I was hopeful when I found a book that I thought might help me. It was entitled "How to Win Over Depression" by Tim LaHaye (1974). I wasn't sure if what I was dealing with was depression but I knew it had to have something to do with the mental torment I was living with. I was afraid to talk to anyone about what I was feeling. I was sure that I was crazy and would be shipped off to a psych ward, to be forgotten and abandoned. It all seems irrational now but at the time I wasn't thinking rationally as my anxiety blew everything out of proportion and far from logical reasoning.

What I learned through that little book was that our thoughts do have an impact on how we feel and that we can learn to choose our thoughts. Up until that point, I had no idea that some thoughts are healthy, some are unhealthy, and that we have the power to guide our thoughts. I learned to stop myself when my thoughts were going in a negative direction, and replace them with positive thoughts. At that time in my life I didn't think I had much to feel positive about (although I did but couldn't see it) so I literally forced myself to focus on anything that was good, such as a flower, a color, a good smell, a nice person, a painting, or anything, absolutely anything that was pleasant or good. Slowly I retrained my brain to steer itself away from the negative thoughts and move toward positive ones. Little by little my anxiety and depression lifted. It took a long time and a lot of hard, persistent work. It's probably the hardest work I have ever done, but it turned my life around at a time when I had few other options or resources, no knowledge of medications to treat anxiety, and no one that I felt I could talk to.

Now I work with clients to help them learn to identify their negative thoughts and beliefs, and replace them with more realistic and positive thoughts. It is based on Cognitive Behavioral Therapy which has been found to be very effective in treating depression and anxiety. Thousands of people have benefitted from this type of therapy and have learned that their feelings are the result of their thoughts and mindset.

We're taught as we grow up how to feed ourselves, how to read and write, how to add and subtract, and how to do many things, but somehow we aren't taught how to think. It just happens, without our realizing it. We perceive and interpret the world around us in very personal ways, and the events in our lives give us opportunities to see those events in one way or another. We may become very critical of others, or overly critical of ourselves. Without realizing it, over time we can set ourselves up for a mental illness. When we think about it, how could we NOT succumb to depression or anxiety if our constant thoughts are negative and focused on worst-case scenarios?

Cognitive Distortions

There are several common distortions that we engage in without realizing it. Although our thoughts seem to be true and accurate, often there are some distortions involved. Here are a few of the most common cognitive distortions:

-**All-or-nothing thinking**: Things are either all bad or all good. If you don't perform well on one task, you see yourself as a total failure.

-**Catastrophizing:** We expect most things to end in a catastrophe, making mountains out of molehills. If your car won't start one morning, you automatically think you'll lose your job, you'll end up homeless, etc.

-**Filtering**: We only see what we want to see and focus on the negative aspects while denying the positive aspects of a situation or person.

-**Overgeneralization**: We come to some general conclusions based on one negative event. If we didn't get the last job, we're sure we'll never get a job.

-**Emotional Reasoning**: If we feel a certain way, we believe it to be reality. If we feel stupid, we think it must be true.

William James, a well-known psychologist and philosopher in the late 1800's and early 1900's said *"The greatest discovery of my generation is that a human being can alter his life by altering his attitudes".*

Besides the influence of our thoughts on our mental wellbeing, other factors also play a role in mental illness, such as our brain chemistry and heredity. We will look at those factors in later chapters.

Homework:

Take a few days to notice your thoughts. Keep a notebook handy and write down the repetitive thoughts you have. What thoughts about yourself are frequent? What patterns do you notice? What is the main focus of your thoughts? How do you feel as you engage in some of those negative thoughts?

Now notice if your feelings or attitudes change when you engage in positive thoughts. Do you feel better, even if just for a moment as you're focusing your mind on something positive?

Look at the list of cognitive distortions. Are you engaging in any of these distortions? Which ones plague you the most?

Which thoughts do you struggle with the most? Are they truth-based? Are they a product of your imagination? Are they fear based? What connections can you make between what you're thinking and how you feel? Can you see the relationship between what you think and your anxiety?

4. *The Power of Visualization and Imagery*

Our imagination is a wonderful gift from God. It is one of our greatest assets, as we can imagine how we want to decorate our home, compose a song, how to design a wooden bench, construct a building, or paint a masterpiece. Without our imagination, nothing that man has made or designed would be in existence. Everything that has ever been created began in the mind of an individual through their imagination. What a gift!

On the other side of the coin, our imagination can be one of our greatest enemies. What we can imagine in our mind feels very real, and consequently, if we imagine something horrible or tragic, our emotions will feel as it the terrible event is actually happening, and our bodies will respond likewise. Our adrenaline shoots up and we feel panic and tension, as if the tragic event is a reality. If you imagine yourself falling off a high cliff, your palms will probably get sweaty, your heart rate will speed up, and you may feel shortness of breath as you imagine falling to your doom. As you can see, what you imagine sets your body in motion as if the event were really happening.

Authors Hirsh and Holmes (2007) state that "anxious imagery often relates to a memory of an earlier aversive or traumatic situation, but the clients experience it as if it is happening in the 'here and now'" (p.161). This also applies to fearful events we can imagine taking place in the future. Our amygdala reacts as if the event is happening to us right then and there. It doesn't know the difference between what's real and what's only taking place in our imagination.

Even though we know in our heads that it's just a mental image, our body doesn't necessarily know that. For this reason, our imagination has to be trained and reined in at times, just as our thoughts do. We can allow our imagination to work for us, or against us. I compare it to a toddler who wants to wander around and can easily go to dangerous places. When my little brother was about two, we lived on a busy street. Someone came to visit and when they left, we didn't realize that the front door wasn't completely closed. Danny ventured out of the house and we found him on the sidewalk near the busy street! Mom quickly scooped him up and ran back inside to safety. His little toddler feet could take him places that were not safe and were dangerous to his wellbeing. Our imagination can take us to many unpleasant and dangerous places, and we must be vigilant to keep it in safe places, just as we have to keep a toddler from going to dangerous places. Just as we say "No Son, you can't go there, come over here and let's look at something else", we can tell our imaginations "no, we're not going there. We're going to imagine something much better now".

In the past when I have been in potentially fearful situations, such as when I was invited to speak to a large group at the First Congress of Christian Counselors in Guadalajara Mexico, my mind could imagine a very fearful situation where the audience was critical and I imagined myself fumbling for words and panicking. As I imagined the upcoming speaking engagement, I could let myself get into a very anxious place! I have learned the value of telling my imagination "No, we're not going there" and instead imagining the best possible outcome. If we can imagine the worst case scenario, we can also imagine the best case scenario. Unfortunately we're more prone to imagine the worst. In the case of the conference in Mexico, I made myself practice daily the image of giving the seminar with confidence, feeling a connection with the participants, and walking away feeling good about my talk. The more I imagined this scenario, the less anxiety I felt prior to flying to Mexico, and the conference was a great experience. I had imagined the positive outcome so much in my mind prior to the trip that it accomplished two things: My anxiety level decreased significantly in the weeks leading up to the conference, and because I had mentally practiced the event with a positive outcome so many times, it went off exactly the way I had imagined it would   Another example of this concept is when athletes train for an upcoming sporting event. They practice for hours, doing the very thing that they hope to do at the event. They do it over and over, practicing for hours. When the event takes place, they're much more likely to perform the way they hope to, due to the practice before the event.

How we see events and situations

As we think about situations, we create a mental image of that situation, one that although we know is not real, feels very real. In a study of the use of positive imagery to positively impact anxiety, Arnaud Pictet (2014) states that "mental imagery has been demonstrated to elicit stronger emotions than other forms of processing. This evocative power has further been shown to apply to both positive and negative emotions, leading to the suggestion that mental imagery may act as an 'emotional amplifier'".

Stopa and Jenkins (2007) found that study participants who gave a speech while focusing on a positive mental image were less anxious than those who gave the speech while holding a negative image.

Here's an example of how my imagination worked against me at one time in my life:

I have flown all my life and as a child I didn't feel nervous about flying at all. It was a big adventure! However, in my late teens, I heard on the news about the terrible PanAm accident where hundreds of passengers died. From then on when I had to fly, I got extremely nervous. As an adult I knew that I didn't want to stop traveling because I love to travel and my job at the time required some travel, but I hated how I felt when the date of the trip approached, and especially when I was finally on the plane! I resorted to taking tranquilizers at times, and toughed it out other times, with my heart pounding, my palms sweating, and feeling as though I couldn't breathe.

I began to analyze what I was thinking surrounding the topic of air travel, and I realized that I was imagining the worst. Every time we hit turbulence during a flight, I imagined one of the airplane wings falling off, or an engine catching fire, or an explosion...and then down, down, down we went, with screams of sheer terror, all the way down, until we hit the ground and exploded in flames. No wonder my internal alarm system was going off! I was creating a tragic scene in my mind and my body was responding as if it were really happening. When we imagine tragic events, our bodies react as if they were real.

In an attempt to reverse this fear, I decided to stay away from the dreaded image in my mind of the plane going down, and I create a different scene. I imagined a few bumps during the flight, but then landing safely, getting my luggage, and hugging my loved ones who were waiting. I imagined all the fun things we would do once I arrived at my destination and the great times with family or friends. Guess what? It worked! I changed the scene in my mind from a tragic one to a happy one, and my body responded by feeling calm and confident.

Homework:

Ask yourself what kind of "movies" you're playing in your mind. Are you imagining the worst-case scenario? Do you allow yourself to see a tragic ending to many events? How does your body respond to those images? It may be time to become aware of the scenes that you're allowing your imagination to paint in your head, and create some better scenes to focus on.

List some of the mental images you have created for yourself. Then create images of a better outcome for those same situations.

How we see ourselves

The image that we have of ourselves, our "self-image" can play a significant role in creating our anxiety and in perpetuating it. Here's what I mean:

If a person feels that they are not capable of facing life's challenges, when the challenges come, they will feel inadequate, small and vulnerable. Imagine being face to face with a giant, with no weapons or means of defense! Would you become anxious? I certainly would! Not only do we tend to see life's challenges as huge, we also see ourselves as tiny and defenseless. We think we're weak and unable to manage stressful situations. We don't have confidence in our ability to handle anything...and before we know it we're in a full blown panic attack or shaking in our boots.

Perhaps our feelings of inadequacy stem from past failures or perhaps from few opportunities to test our abilities and see that we ARE in fact capable of dealing with life. One of the mistakes that some parents make is to solve their children's problems, and shield them from all difficult situations. Some mothers run to their child's school over and over throughout their elementary years, to solve their child's problems with other classmates or teachers. They never allow their child to deal with things, thus giving the child the sense that they aren't capable of dealing with the tough stuff when it comes. Protecting our children has to be balanced with allowing them to stick up for themselves, being resourceful and becoming resilient in the face of adversity. This can lead to an adult who has little confidence in his or her ability to deal with life's tough events. This adult may see themselves as weak and powerless.

Once we are trapped in the vicious cycle of anxiety, we may begin to see ourselves as "sick", "losers" or "worthless", and the more we view ourselves this way, the less capable we will feel to deal with our illness. Many individuals feel completely hopeless in overcoming their anxiety, because they see themselves as mentally ill, incompetent and useless. This can actually become a self-fulfilling prophecy, that maintains us stuck in a very bad place.

The key is to stop seeing ourselves as weak and sick, and although we can be fully aware that we are dealing with an anxiety disorder, we should also be aware that we ARE capable of overcoming it and getting to a much better place. When I began to put this into practice I immediately turned a corner in my recovery. I no longer saw myself as sick, and I began to look at the internal resources that I knew I possessed, such as resilience, stubbornness (yes, it's a great quality to possess in times like these!), and determination.

Homework:

Practice closing your eyes for 3-5 minutes two times a day, and imagine yourself well, free of the anxiety. Remember a time in your life when you were anxiety free. Remember a time when you felt confident and in control of your life. Then imagine yourself in the future, free of anxiety. Visualize how you feel, what your life looks like, how you handle challenges. Stay in that frame of mind for a few minutes. Then smile and tell yourself that you WILL get there. You WILL be free of the anxiety and your life will be what you want it to be. Hold the smile for a few more minutes.

There is power in seeing ourselves the way that we want to be! The more we visualize something, the more we hold that image in our minds, the more we move toward it. I encourage you to make a habit of setting aside time each day to do this homework.

Using Imagery to calm ourselves

Imagery and visualization have long been used to remain calm in stressful situations. It can be used on a regular basis to bring peace and tranquility to our minds. It involves finding a quiet, comfortable place, sitting or lying down, closing our eyes, and imagining a place or scene that brings us peace. My peaceful place is the beach in Venezuela where I lived for many years. In reality the beaches there are beautiful but not always peaceful due to the crowds of people, the loud music and the constant parade of salesmen offering ice cream, seafood, hats, toys, and all sorts of things. In my peaceful place though, I'm at the beach alone, lying in my hammock stretched between two coconut trees. I can hear the waves, see the blue and aqua tones of the water, smell the sea breeze…I look up from my hammock and see the coconut tree branches swaying in the breeze. Not only do I visualize the sights and sounds of my place, but I also imagine the feelings of peace and contentment that I feel there. I smile as I visualize my place, and relax into it.

I stay in this peaceful state as long as I want to, until I'm ready to get up and get back to whatever I need to be doing next. Another image that I use is a rose. I love flowers, and visualizing a rose, its color and texture, rain drops on its petals, and the joy that I feel upon inhaling its aroma brings me peace.

This exercise of going to our peaceful place, and imagining something beautiful and good, isn't simply "fluff", or some well-meaning psychologist's simplistic idea. They actually improve our brain's chemistry and they help to "grow" new neural pathways. Medical imaging (fMRI) has proven this fact. Positive changes in the brain can actually be seen! This is exciting to me, because now we have the science to prove what we have suspected for years: Filling our minds with positive, peaceful images actually heals our brains. The more we practice positive imagery, the better our brains function.

Homework:

Find a quiet place in your home or outdoors and sit or lie down. Breathe deeply and relax your muscles. Close your eyes and find your peaceful place. Imagine the sights, the colors, the smells, the sounds of this place. Spend time focusing on each of these. Think about why you like this place so much. Smile as you enjoy your peaceful place. Relax your body and "sink into" your place. Create feelings of peace and contentment in your place. Stay in this place for 10-15 minutes, two or three times a day, or as needed.

5. The Power of Refocusing

One of the best strategies I found for dealing with anxiety was to stop trying to deal with it! The very nature of anxiety leads us to focus constantly on the anxiety itself, hoping to fix it, make it go away, or find a solution. We would like to find the magic formula that ends the obsessing and anguish. As we look for the solution, we end up ruminating and obsessing about our anxiety disorder or panic disorder even more. Trying to fix it doesn't work and only adds fuel to the fire. The more we try to figure out how to rid ourselves of this problem with anxiety, the more it grows. I mentioned earlier that I felt like a hamster on a running wheel, and that is exactly what it feels like. The harder we try to get rid of the anxiety, the worse it gets. The original issue that caused our anxiety is long forgotten and we're now several layers deep in our own self-created angst. We end up exhausted and depleted emotionally. There have been few times in my life that I have been as exhausted as when I had a panic disorder and spent every waking moment trying to figure it out, find the solution and make it go away! I was weary from dealing with it for several months, but it persisted and I continued to focus on getting rid of the anxiety. Looking back I don't know how I managed to function somewhat normally as a wife and mother of two children. It was as if someone had flipped a switch in my brain and I was in another mode altogether, and that mode was anxiety-ridden, 24/7, and the quest for a "cure" was all-consuming. I analyzed myself, my reasons for being anxious, I obsessed over my physical symptoms, and I just dug myself deeper and deeper in the hole.

Paradoxically, if we really want to reduce our anxiety, we must stop trying to reduce it! When we feel those anxious feelings, whether in our thoughts or in physical sensations, we should recognize the feelings, accept them, and move our focus to something else...anything else!

> *When we feel anxiety in any form, it is always best to switch our attention EXTERNALLY as much as possible. Our feelings lie to us when they involve anxiety, so it's best to take our attention away from our internal*

anxiety feelings (take away their power) by focusing on any sounds, sights, or other external stimuli that you can think of... There is nothing to "figure out" about anxiety... it is just there, and it will continue to be there unless you can remove attention from it and get

your mind moving in a positive/neutral direction... The less "importance" we can place on our anxiety feelings / thoughts, the less they will have the power to control us, and the less upset we will get by any perceived setbacks or overwhelming anxiety feelings we experience. Focus externally, stay active, exercise, work out at the gym... do anything to take your attention away from anxiety, and stop fueling the fire. Contrary to what you may believe, analysis of your inner anxiety feelings will get you NOWHERE. It will only create more anxiety in your life, and it will become even more difficult to break free of it in the future. Anxiety can only harm you when you focus inward and pay attention to it, so let's get our minds moving in a positive direction on some external,

positive events / situations. You WILL notice an
immediate difference, and if you practice this enough,
you will experience a better and brighter tomorrow.
(socialanxietyinstitute.org)

I have found that when I feel anxiety, shifting my focus from my anxiety to something positive and external immediately lessens the anxiety. It is difficult to do, because the very nature of anxiety demands that we focus inward and on the feelings we're experiencing. We can spend hours, days, weeks and months trying to "deal" with the anxiety, only to find that we're still stuck in the box, still spinning our wheels. No amount of thinking will rid us of anxiety! The only thing that really works is to focus on other things. I remember grasping for ANYTHING to focus on besides myself, my feelings, and my inner turmoil. Sometimes I focused on the blue color of the sky. Other times I thought about a flower, or a puppy, or a rainbow. I would scan my surroundings and find something to observe and then notice every detail. I tried to find something positive in each thing that I focused on, and this helped. It was certainly better than focusing on how bad I felt, which made me feel worse.

In a way, we could say that dealing with anxiety involves counterintuitive strategies, or paradoxical strategies. We logically think that we should focus on the anxiety in order to figure it out and banish it, right? In this case, focusing on it only makes it stronger. The less we focus on our feelings, and the more we focus on anything outside of ourselves and our feelings, the more peace we will feel.

It doesn't happen overnight, and it doesn't happen on its own. Remember that our anxiety will try its best to keep us focused on it. In a way, it's like a spoiled child, demanding attention! The best thing we can do is consistently refocus our attention on anything BUT the anxiety, over and over, until those neural pathways are depleted and defeated, and new pathways are created.

Homework:

Ask yourself if you spend much of your time focusing on how you feel, or on ridding yourself of the anxiety, and being very internally focused in general. If so, make a conscious effort to focus on anything outside of yourself. Make a list of things you could focus on other than yourself and keep the list close by, perhaps in your cellphone. Wear a rubber band around your wrist and every time you look at the rubber band, make sure you think about something positive that is external. Get involved in helping someone, either a neighbor or a friend, or do volunteer work in a local non-profit organization. They will appreciate your help and you will become less focused on yourself and how you feel!

6. The Power of "So What" instead of "What if?"

One of the mental patterns that keeps people stuck in their anxiety is the "what if" question that plays in their minds over and over. They automatically think about any situation in the worst-case sense. When they engage in the "what if" question about any given situation, their minds imagine the worst possible outcome. Some examples are "My son is traveling overseas. What if he gets mugged or kidnapped?", "I found a dark spot on my neck...what if it's cancer?", "I'd like to make friends with that lady but what if she makes fun of me and talks about me to her friends?"

As we saw in the chapter on imagery and visualization, what we imagine in our minds feels real and our bodies react to the imagined threat as if it were real. This sets in motion the work of the amygdala, sending signals throughout our body to prepare to fight or flee. At that point we'll feel shortness of breath, rapid heart rate, tingling in the hands or feet, nausea, and many other physical symptoms of anxiety. I used to feel that my throat was closing up and I couldn't swallow. Each person's physical symptoms will vary. Even if we are sitting comfortably in our living room safe from all harm, our bodies might be ready to face the worst possible imagined situation. We then feel crazy for feeling this way and we're sure that no one would understand what's going on in this crazy head of ours.

"What if" can become a very bad and damaging habit that robs us of any peace that we could be enjoying. "What if I die of cancer?", "what if my husband has an accident?", "what if my child gets lost and can't find his way home?", "what if I never get better?", "what if I lose my job, lose my home, and end up homeless?" These are common thoughts for those who suffer from "what-if-itis". No wonder we experience constant anxiety! We're feeding their minds with images of worst case scenarios which fuels our anxiety.

I found an alternative thought that helped me to counteract the "what ifs". It is called the "So what?" attitude. It was hard in the beginning to practice the "so what" mindset, but with practice it took root and I was eventually able to think "So what" anytime a "what if" came into my mind. Practicing "so what" is basically learning to care less about things that might happen, because they usually don't ever become reality.

I'm not advocating that we ignore our responsibilities or stop caring about ourselves and others, but much of anxiety is the result of caring too much. We can care so much about something that we begin to obsess about it. The "so what" attitude helps us to care a little less and to put things into perspective.

I had a friend whose favorite word was "whatever". It was frustrating when I asked her something, and she answered "whatever" as she shrugged her shoulders! I understand now that this might have been her strategy to keep anxiety from taking over. Adopting a "laissez-faire" attitude can help us to focus less on the things that might go wrong and help us to go with the flow. Usually the things we fear never happen, so the "so what" and " whatever" approach is usually appropriate and helpful.

This "so what" outlook may seem uncaring to some. I certainly wouldn't say "so what" to someone who has just shared a personal problem with me. That would be rude and insensitive. The application of "so what" is for my own use in my own inner world, and it helps me to shrug off the "what ifs" as they come into my mind. In a way this way of thinking is giving up control over our life and letting go of the idea that we can prevent bad things from happening if we think about them enough.

There's a saying that I like to share with my clients when we're discussing how to deal with those automatic negative thoughts that pop into our heads throughout the day. I don't remember where I heard it but it's been very useful:

"You can't stop a bird from landing on your head, but you can prevent it from making its nest in your hair".

Homework:

Ask yourself what "What ifs" you regularly entertain in your thoughts. Make of list of the most common ones.

Today start practicing the "so what" attitude. When the "what if" makes its appearance in your thoughts, switch it quickly to "so what". Do this over and over, each time you're tempted to think about a very bad outcome to a situation.

7. The Power of Staying Busy

One of the worst enemies of good mental health is inactivity. When we don't do anything, we tend to ruminate about our real problems, our potential and imagined problems, and then we fixate on the anxiety and its symptoms. This only fuels it! On the other hand, staying busy is one of the most helpful things I have found to deal with anxiety.

I have heard of individuals who are on disability due to their anxiety. I do understand that for some, anxiety is a crippling disease that hasn't been helped by medication or therapy. I wonder at times if those individuals have been diligent with their medication and if they have a good Dr. and counselor who have experience helping patients with anxiety disorders. Even when a person is on disability due to anxiety, they can benefit from staying busy. There is nothing worse for anxiety and depression than doing nothing. It's a recipe for disaster and usually leads to worsening of the condition. When our mind is not occupied with a task or a goal, it will naturally turn to thinking about the difficulties, frustrations and problems we face. Without anything productive to pull us away from our anxious thoughts, they will fester and grow stronger.

Whether a person works or not, it's vital that they stay in contact with others and engage in some activity that helps them feel productive and useful. Volunteering is one effective way to be productive and active. There are countless organizations that need help such as animal shelters, rescue missions, after school programs, church programs, mission trips, soup kitchens, road clean up crews, and so many more! Being engaged in helping others is a powerful way to get our minds off our own problems and get us focused on others. It goes back to the overly internal focus versus the outward focus that we discussed earlier.

Besides volunteering, there are so many other productive things to engage in that will keep our minds active and focused on things other than our own feelings. We can sign up for a class, repaint the bedroom, start exercising, write a novel, sort and organize the closet, visit friends, or clean out the garage. We can go fishing, run errands for a sick friend, go window shopping, learn to play a musical instrument, or plant flowers in the garden. What we do doesn't matter as much as the fact that we just do something!

Sometimes people will say that they didn't do something because they just didn't feel like it. It is hard to get up and do something that we don't feel like doing. Believe me, I know. Today I was thinking that I needed to get up and do some exercise but I just didn't feel like it. Eventually I did get off the sofa and did some exercise. Once I did it, I felt great and was glad I did.

Our feelings will often lead us astray, telling us that we don't feel like doing anything except stay in bed with the covers over our head. We don't feel like facing the world, going to work, working out, visiting a friend, running errands. If we listen to our feelings, we'll become very unproductive and we'll have more time to focus on ourselves and our anxiety. It's imperative that we do what we know we need to do in spite of how we feel! The more active we are, the better we will feel and the less we'll focus on ourselves and our bad feelings. Some therapies recommend acting "as if". In other words, even if you don't feel like going to work, act "as if" you do, and go to work. Once you do this over and over you realize that you can do those things that were holding you back and that going ahead and doing them actually helps you feel better about yourself. There's a feeling of accomplishment that goes with getting things done, and a sense that we are indeed capable of doing important tasks. We'll feel more confident in our ability to face life and live a productive life.

Homework:

What do you need to do today? Write down two things that you could or should do. Stop making excuses, get up, and tackle the first one. Act "as if" you want to do those things, and do them. Take "baby steps" if necessary. A friend who was afraid of driving due to her anxiety began to drive again by driving to the end of the block the first day. Every day thereafter she made herself drive a little further, until she could drive to the market and get her groceries. Baby steps are the way to go.

Afterward: How do you feel after taking care of that first item on your list? Did you do it well? Do you feel satisfied? While you were busy doing it, was your anxiety any better? At least were you able to think about something else during that time? Were you less focused on your anxious thoughts and feelings?

8. *The Power of Positive People and Experiences*

Sometimes life throws so many negative events at us within a short time period that we soon begin to expect more negative things to happen. It seems that when it rains, it pours. Without realizing it, our internal attitudes become so negative that we have a hard time imagining that anything will ever go right again.

My daughter and her husband experienced this, starting a few of years ago. It started with a major move with dishonest movers which cost them several thousand dollars, then a car accident which totaled the car (thankfully no major injuries), a terrible job that ultimately had to be left, another car accident while my daughter was pregnant (thank God no injuries), an emergency C-section, difficulties breast feeding, my son-in-law had ankle surgery and was on crutches or in a boot/cast for several months, another major move, my daughter broke her foot, was in a boot for months and then had foot surgery, more crutches and a boot. Both parents were in boots and on crutches at the same time, while caring for a baby! No one could believe the string of negative events that happened to them, nor could they. They were both worn out both physically and emotionally. Insomnia was a major issue and anxiety became overwhelming at times. Who wouldn't be anxious after so many difficult challenges?

At times I encouraged my daughter to engage in anything that might bring her some joy, even if for a few moments. One sunny day in the fall, we took a quilt outside and spread it on the grass near the back porch. She laid in the sunshine while I chased my granddaughter all over the backyard (she was crawling at that time). Being outdoors and soaking in the sunshine was helpful as it created pleasant sensations and a sense of wellbeing. Seeing a funny movie or joining a friend for a pedicure can provide some moments of joy or relaxation.

Engaging in volunteer work is another experience that is usually positive and rewarding. When we help someone else, we're less focused on ourselves and more focused on others.

Our minds are tied up helping instead of brewing about how we feel and our circumstances.

Positive experiences can be created all around us. Sometimes when I'm in between errands, I sit in my car in a parking lot and watch the birds as they hop around searching for crumbs. I watch as they fly up in the trees and enjoy their snack or take it to their babies in their nest.

I enjoy sunsets and sunrises, especially over the fields in the area where I live. I love to take an early morning drive down highway 112 where the morning mist envelops the cows in the fields and the barns stand against the pink and purple sunrise.

One friend told me that she takes a hot bubble bath when she feels discouraged and frustrated. The experience of relaxing in a tub of hot water helps her to forget about the negative events of the day.

Many people find that being in nature is a great way to create positive experiences. They may take a picnic to enjoy by the river, or hike a new trail. For some, riding on their bike through the park creates a sense of wellbeing. After all, they're healthy enough to ride a bike no matter what their age!

Photography brings joy to many people as they capture beauty on their camera. They don't have to have a nice camera to do so-an iPhone camera will do. The point is to see beauty all around us and to capture that moment to enjoy later or to share with others.

Homework:

What positive experience can you create for yourself? Keep it simple-a bubble bath, a sunset, reading a good book or getting out in nature. Just do it! Every day! Start a log in your notebook of one positive experience a day. It could be something very simple, and it doesn't matter as long as it's positive. What will you do today?

Positive People

We all know plenty of negative people, don't we? There are the ones who are constantly complaining, others who gossip about their friends, the family member who drag us down into their pit, the people who always need something from us that we can't give. There are those who try to abuse our kindness and push our buttons. There are drama queens and party poopers and the ones who're never satisfied. If we're not careful, we can quickly become surrounded by negative people and their negativity is contagious. When I lived in Venezuela, I hated going to the doctor's office for two reasons: First, appointments were unheard of so patients showed up and waited your turn. This could easily turn into a 3-4 hour wait (no exaggeration)! The second reason I hated it was that the people in the waiting room seemed to have a habit of comparing their "gloom and doom stories" of their physical ailments. Each person tried to outdo the previous person, telling the awful details of the operations and procedures they had been through. Even if I was at the doctor's office for a checkup or something minor, I usually left 3 or 4 hours later feeling very sick, mostly from hearing all the "woe is me" muck around me. I do feel compassion for those who are sick, but hearing all the details of everyone's health problems made me sicker than I was already!

If we want to become more positive in the way that we see the world and how we see ourselves, it's essential to surround ourselves with positive people! There's never a shortage of negative people, but where are the positive people? Sadly, the truth is that it's not always easy to find positive people to associate with. It takes some effort on our part, and staying home alone usually will not help us meet positive people. Even if we don't feel like it, it's important to put ourselves out there where we can meet positive people. Where can we meet good people who give off good vibes? There are good people everywhere but there are certain places that we may be more likely to meet them: exercise classes, craft classes, mother's groups, church groups or Bible studies, yoga and meditation classes, neighborhood groups, community groups, support groups. There are photography clubs, hiking groups, and activist groups. These are just a few of the places where you might meet some interesting and positive people.

Positive people have a beneficial effect on us for several reasons. They remind us of all that's good in the world around us. They also believe the best in others, which includes us. They are good at encouraging us when we're down and they see our virtues. Their perspective on life is completely different from negative people and their optimism is contagious (just as negativity is contagious). They radiate hope and faith in God and the human race and this hope can help us to feel better despite our circumstances. Positive people aren't immune to life's struggles, and usually they've been through some incredible challenges themselves, but they came out on top and can attest to the fact that recovery from your struggle with anxiety is possible and probable. Many positive people are positive because they have an unwavering faith in God and they believe in His goodness, even in the face of life's difficulties. They're not positive because their life has been easy or free of difficulties-in fact usually they have weathered the storms and become more resilient.

One person comes to mind when I think about positive people: "Juan". At a shopping center that I went to frequently in Venezuela, there was a young man in a wheel chair at the parking lot exit. He had a stack of newspapers on his lap and he sold them to patrons as they exited the parking lot. Juan had lost his legs in an accident, yet he smiled every day and earned a living selling newspapers. He had plenty of reasons to be negative but he was one of the most positive people I have ever met. Juan knew about adversity. He knew about pain, and he knew about loss. He had not only lost his legs but he lost his independence. A family member drove him to the shopping center every day and helped him get set up in his wheel chair and newspapers. I never saw Juan that he wasn't smiling and greeting those who passed by. What an inspiration!

Homework:

Who are the positive people in your life? Who helps you to believe in yourself and reminds you that you will feel better soon? Who encourages you and who reminds you of God's goodness and faithfulness? Who do you need to reach out to and stay connected to?

If you don't have such people in your life, where can you go to associate yourself with positive people? What's the first step in making connections with positive people? What can you commit to today to make connections with them?

9. The Power of Medication and Supplements

There are several things I would like to discuss that pertain to our physical health as it relates to our recovery from anxiety. The first one is the importance of vitamins and minerals for optimal brain functioning, and the second one is the need for medication for some individuals.

Our brains are organs just like our heart, lungs, kidneys and liver. As such they require certain nutrients to function at their best. I'm not a medical doctor nor a pharmacist but I will share what I have learned over the years about the supplements that are vital to our brain's health.

Supplements:

The supplement that I recommend the most is Omega3. A study conducted at Ohio State University Center for Clinical and Translational Science, and published in the journal *Brain, Behavior and Immunity* found that Omega 3 reduces anxiety and inflammation in healthy individuals. Previous investigation demonstrated that Omega 3 can reduce depression and levels of cytokines in the body which are responsible for inflammation.

Vitamin D is important for our mental health, and it can be absorbed through sunshine. Some individuals suffer more during the winter months due to a lack of sunshine and vitamin D and sun lamps are sometimes used to provide vitamin D. It can also be taken in tablet form although the natural source through sunshine is always best. I recommend that my clients go outside at least 10 minutes a day if the weather permits, and soak up some rays!

The B vitamins are important for the health of our nerves. B1, thiamine, helps to protect the immune system and helps us deal with stress. B6 is important as we consider supplements that can help alleviate anxiety, as it helps the body produce serotonin, melatonin and norepinephrine. B9 can help prevent depression and promote healthy memory.

Magnesium is an important mineral that plays an important role in the body's biochemical processes. Current

RDA requirement of Magnesium is 320-420 mg per day and most people consume less than that. This deficiency can lead to anxiety, depression, headaches, irritability and other negative consequences. Stress depletes our levels of Magnesium, just when our bodies seem to need it the most! It also acts at the blood brain barrier to hinder the entrance of stress hormones into the brain. Calcium and glutamate live in the synapses between neurons and they are both excitatory. Magnesium also sits there with calcium and glutamate and it "guards" them from become too active. When magnesium is deficient, calcium and glutamate have no "guardian" and can run wild, thus producing more anxiety.

Medications:

Medications are often prescribed by physicians to aid in alleviating anxiety. One class of drugs that is commonly prescribed is benzodiazepines. These medications are known as anti-anxiety drugs or tranquilizers. They work quickly in reducing anxious symptoms, usually within a half hour. The down side is that these medications are addictive if taken for a long time. This is not to say that they shouldn't be prescribed and used, because they do have their place. When a person is extremely anxious and cannot think straight or function normally, a tranquilizer such as Xanax or Ativan can provide relief. The key is to weigh the advantages and disadvantages of taking this type of medication, and striving to take the lowest possible dose for the shortest period of time.

Another useful type of medication that is useful in treating anxiety is the anti-depressant. An anxious person might argue that they aren't depressed, only anxious, and thus do not need an antidepressant. The word "depression" is often misleading and conjures up images of a person crying and lying in bed all day.

The fact is that most anxious individuals' brain chemistry is depressed, or to put in another way, it's lazy or sluggish. Antidepressants help the brain to get back on track, and promote a sense of wellbeing. SSRI's, or Selective Serotonin Reuptake Inhibitors work by inhibiting the reuptake of serotonin just as the name expresses. Our neurons produce serotonin which helps to relay messages on down the chain of neurons, but sometimes the same neuron that produces the serotonin reaches out and takes it back! This leads then to a decrease in the amount of serotonin that should be moving along from neuron to neuron. SSRI's seek to stop or slow down the reuptake process, thus freeing up the serotonin to do its job. Some commonly prescribed SSRIs are Zoloft, Prozac, and Paxil.

Newer generations of antidepressants work in similar ways, although some work on different neurotransmitters, but they all have the potential to restore the brain's chemistry and functioning. Some of the newer antidepressants are Lexapro, Wellbutrin, Cymbalta, among others. Many of the newer antidepressants have fewer side effects than the SSRIs and certainly than older, first generation tricyclic antidepressants. Some of these work not only on serotonin but also on other neurotransmitters that are involved in anxiety and depression.

Natural Antidepressants:

There are several natural antidepressants available and some individuals choose to try the natural options before resorting to medication. One of these is St. John's Wort (Hypericum perforatum) and it has been used for decades. St. John's Wort also acts as an anti-inflammatory, antiviral and helps digestion. St. John's Wort can interact with other medications, therefore consultation with a physician is a must.

5-HTP is another natural antidepressant that works by providing the body with what it needs to produce serotonin. In other words, it's the raw material needed for production of serotonin. 5-HTP has been used successfully by thousands of individuals to treat depression and anxiety.

SAM-e, or S-adenosylmethionine, is a naturally occurring chemical in the body based on the animo acid methionine. It boosts several neurotransmitters and can influence healthy nerve conduction. It has been useful to alleviate joint pain.

Fortunately today there are physicians who are not only knowledgeable about medications, but also about supplements and natural remedies that can help a person with anxiety and depression. It is well worth looking for such a provider in order to discuss and choose the best option.

New Strategies:

Recently a new device, the Fisher Wallace stimulator, has been made available to the general public. The general idea of the device is to gently stimulate the brain's production of serotonin and other neurotransmitters that might be lacking, through gentle electrical impulses, transmitted through pads placed on the temples. While this may sound "hocus pocus" some individuals have found relief. I believe we are on the verge of several breakthroughs in alternative treatments to anxiety and depression, which should give us a feeling of hope for future generations as they deal with anxiety.

Homework:

Take inventory of the supplements that you take and decide if you need to add any of the supplements I have mentioned. Give it time to make a difference! It can take 2-4 weeks to feel the positive effects.

Talk to your Dr. about medications if you haven't already. If your Dr. has only prescribed tranquilizers, ask about the possibility of adding an antidepressant or a natural antidepressant. If so, give it time, and be prepared for some of the side-effects to show up during the first couple of weeks. The side-effects will usually decrease the longer the medication is used and the benefits of the antidepressant will be felt within 2 to 4 weeks.

10.The Power of a Sense of Wellbeing

As you know by now, one of the things missing in your life is an overall sense of wellbeing. Most sufferers of an anxiety disorder feel exhausted all the time, even if they get a good night's sleep. They may have stomach troubles as well as headaches and a host of other ailments. A feeling of doom is pervasive and a sense of wellbeing has been absent for months or years.

One of the things I encourage my clients to do is to cultivate that sense of wellbeing. It doesn't happen overnight, and the anxious feelings are well entrenched. Our negative neural pathways seem like they're set in stone, and getting out of that negative mode is difficult, but not impossible. I liken it to a memory I have of going to the beautiful beaches in Venezuela. Parque Nacional Morrocoy has about 28 islands off the northern coast, and fishing boats take tourists and vacationers to the island of their choice. One of our favorite islands had a beach on the backside of the island where the boat docked, but the best beach was on the front side of the island which faced the open sea. In order to get from one side of the island to the other, we had to walk down a long path which took about 15-20 minutes. The path was well used, as many people preferred the beach on the front side of the island, but the problem was that many people also used that path as a "bathroom". Walking the path was like a minefield as we dodged the "smelly piles" left by previous tourists. One day when we arrived at the island I decided that I would no longer go down that nasty path to get to the nicest beach on the other side of the island. My husband insisted that we stick to the worn path. It was already there and it was clear to find our way to the other beach. However I refused to continue down the smelly path and decided I would cut a new path to the other side. Needless to say, it was very tough work! I didn't have any garden tools or machete to cut through the brush, but I forged on. I felt like giving up sometimes and I was tempted to return to the old path. When I thought of the "public bathroom" of the old path, I renewed my resolve to cut a new path. It took me a long, long time, perhaps over an hour, but eventually I got to the nice beach. My husband was already there since he had taken the old path which took him 15 minutes. I was worn out, but happy that I had forged a new path!

The point of this story is that our thoughts want to take the easy way out, the path of least resistance, which is usually the negative route which leads us to more and more feelings of anxiety or depression (or both). If we continue to allow ourselves to think the way we've been thinking, we'll continue to feel the way we feel. The only way to get out of the vicious cycle is to "cut a new path" in our brains. We have to redouble our efforts to find and think thoughts that are peaceful, lovely and helpful. We'll be tempted over and over during the day, especially during the first few weeks, to give up and go back to our well known ways of thinking. If we let our guard down and stop actively working on our new pathways, we'll find ourselves on the old path, thinking the familiar, frightening thoughts that got us in in trouble in the first place.

Meditation is a great way to forge new pathways, when we meditate on positive images, beautiful scenes, happy memories, feelings of accomplishments, people we love, puppies and kittens. It really doesn't matter what the content of the meditation is as long as it's positive and gives us a good feeling.

Once we have those thoughts in our minds, we can search for the positive feelings that go with them, and hold on to them, expand them, enjoy them. We thus create our own sense of wellbeing.

Homework:

Think about this and write your answers in your notebook: What old paths have you allowed your mind to wander down? What are your common, self-defeating thoughts that keep you stuck?

Now find some happy memories, some accomplishments you're proud of, a person you love, or a pet that's warm and fuzzy. Close your eyes and focus on that image. Feel the warmth, the peace, the pride, the joy. Enjoy the feelings, and hold on to them. When they wane, go back to your memory or thought, and feel the joy again and again. Take your time with these thoughts and feelings. Bask in their glow. Don't rush them away to get on with other thoughts or pending tasks.

Other ways to experience a sense of wellbeing

There are many things that contribute to our feelings of wellbeing. One is striving daily to become more healthy. We may feel that we're a long way from being healthy, but even the smallest effort each day can help us feel that we're becoming healthier and promote our sense of wellbeing. If you don't exercise, start today! Start by walking, not running. Don't overdo it. Do some sit-ups or stretches. Do these every day, and as you do them, think about how you're getting healthier. Pat yourself on the back! Tell yourself you're doing a great job!

Go outside, weather permitting, and enjoy some sunshine. Take several deep breaths, inhaling slowly, holding it, and then exhaling slowly. Feel the sun on your face, feel the warmth and energy it provides. Hold thoughts of gratitude in your mind as you enjoy the sun's rays and breathe in health and joy.

You can also commit to eating healthier foods. Begin with small steps. If you drink sodas, eliminate those from your eating habits. After a week or two, you'll see that you don't miss them. You may find that you've lost weight! Sugary drinks are the enemy of mental health, as well as desserts and most sweets. Next, start incorporating more vegetables in your diet. Fortunately these days there are so many choices, from fresh vegetables to frozen ones that are easily steamed in the microwave and ready to eat in just minutes. If you don't already, set a goal of eating two vegetables per day. Then add fruit to your daily nutrition, and then focus on eating more protein (meat, fish, eggs). The best meal includes some protein, vegetables, and good fats. There are many great books and programs that outline a healthy, balanced eating plan, so I won't go into that here. The main point is that our poor eating habits contribute to feeling unhealthy physically and mentally, and good eating habits lead us to be and feel more healthy.

Developing relationships with positive people is something we have already looked at in chapter 8. The truth is that as we relate to others in healthy ways, sharing our feelings and thoughts with them, expressing what we need from the relationship, respecting their feelings and needs, and enjoying activities with them, we mutually contribute to each others' sense of wellbeing. We thrive when we're part of a healthy relationship.

Being a part of a group, a community or church can help us develop feelings of wellbeing as well. Humans were created to be in healthy relationships and to be a part of a group. I believe that many anxious people feel disconnected and alone, and this can contribute to even more anxiety. Who will they turn to when a need arises? Who can they talk to when they feel lonely? Who will check on them periodically? What a gift it is to be a part of a group where others check in and ask how we're doing! There are many groups that happen naturally such as our work colleagues, or church members if we attend church. There are also groups related to hobbies or classes that we might belong to like a rock climbing club or cycling group. Mothers of Preschoolers is an excellent group for those with little ones at home, and there are many other "mommy" groups as well as "daddy" groups. There are support groups, therapy groups, and many online groups. The more connected we are to others, the more supported and healthy we feel.

Another tool I recommend to my clients is to do something nice for themselves daily. A small act of kindness to oneself is never wasted! It doesn't have to involved spending money either. Some examples of things I do for myself are:

-Sit on the deck and watch the sunset.

-Watch an episode of my favorite series.

-Call a friend to chat.

-Give myself a facial.

-Eat a piece of chocolate (only one).

-Take a bubble bath after a long day.

-Take a nap.

-Read from my favorite book.

-Get some exercise.

    -Write in my journal.

This list will look different for each person, and it doesn't matter what you do as long as you're taking care of yourself. Just as we should show kindness to others, we should also show kindness to ourselves.

Homework:

Do you exercise daily? How much? Do you need to begin exercising? What is your plan?

What about your eating habits? What do you need to eliminate or add to your nutrition? How will you do that?

Which people are you connected to, and how do they contribute to your sense of belonging and wellbeing? How can you deepen those relationships?

What groups are you a part of? Are they edifying and healthy? Do you need to join another group? Begin by investigating the groups in your area or online that interest you. Find out when and where they meet. If the thought of going alone produces more anxiety, ask a friend to go with you the first time.

Make a list of things you can do for yourself every day, little acts of kindness that say "I care about you". Choose one to do today and be creative in finding new ways to care for yourself.

11. The Power of Gratitude

I have found that gratitude is one of the best antidotes to anxiety and depression. This is because when we're grateful, we're focused on the positive things in life and the blessings that we're able to enjoy. The Bible teaches us to "be grateful in everything" and instructs us to give thanks at least 73 times.

When we practice gratitude regularly we actually create new neuropathways in our brains and the older less positive pathways are eventually weakened. The brain is "plastic", meaning that it can reroute itself, rewire itself, and reinvent itself. This is why patients who have suffered a stroke or a Traumatic Brain Injury (TBI) and have lost certain functions are often able to regain those functions, using other areas of their brains. The brain is an amazing organ and can work for us when we guide it and feed it the right input.

Being grateful is the perfect way to "get outside of our heads" and focus on all the things that are going right in our lives and around us.

Some people ask "what do I have to be grateful for?" At first glance they may not find anything worthy of gratitude. I urge my clients to take a second look and truly strive to find things to be grateful for. Here is a list of simple things to be grateful for, it could go on and on: The gift of eyesight, taste, hearing, and touch. Feet that work to get us where we need to go, hands that can lift object and help us feed ourselves. A digestive system that works well (most of the time), a heart that beats without having to command it to beat, lungs that breath in air and send oxygen to every part of our body. A country where we're free to choose our profession, find jobs, work and earn a living, family members who care about us, friends, intelligence (more or less!), talents and gifts, the blue sky, water (I love water in all its forms!), sand, beaches, palm trees, animals (dogs in particular), flowers, sunsets.

This is just the tip of the iceberg as there are so many more things to be grateful for.

Homework:

Start a gratitude list. Every day add three things that you're grateful for. Try to be creative and think of things you may not have ever given much thought to previously.

12.The Power of God's Healing

I believe that in addition to all the strategies I've already covered, we have an additional resource which is the greatest of all: The power of God's healing. God wants His children to be at peace, even in the middle of difficult circumstances and challenges, including dealing with an anxiety disorder. Sometimes God chooses to heal a person miraculously and instantly, and sometimes he chooses to make the process of healing a journey. The journey is often long and exhausting, but many lessons are learned along the way. As we learn that we can't make this disorder "go away", we realize that we MUST rely on God's strength and love to see us through. His strength is like a mighty tailwind that pushes us onward and upward as we learn to let go of the anxiety and the desire to control the outcomes of our life. He himself gives us many strategies and tools to use in this journey: Focusing our minds on the good things in life (Philippians 4:8), being grateful (I Thes. 5:18), and thinking less about ourselves and more about others (I Cor. 10:24). He instructs us to renew our minds (Romans 12:2) and to bring every thought captive (2 Cor. 10:5). As we put these tools into practice, we find that we're less concerned about ourselves and more aware of others and of His presence around us.

Focusing on God's attributes is also an effective way to relieve anxiety. I attended a church in Ft. Worth many years ago and the pastor preached a series on God's attributes. As we learned about God's power, His great love for us, His knowledge of everything that happens in our lives, His plan for the world and for each of us, His presence all around us and in us, and the fact that He will never abandon us, we're able to grow in our ability to live our lives with confidence that He is in control and we don't have to control everything ourselves.

Even if you're not a church goer and you're not into organized religion, thinking about a Higher Being who is benevolent and knows every detail of your life can bring peace to your mind. This might be a good time to learn more about God and find a group of people who believe in His love to encourage you and help you grow.

Helpful Scriptures

In the Bible, Jesus tells us not to worry, and reminds us that the birds don't worry, even though they spend most of their waking moments searching for food. Few of us have to spend our entire day looking for food to sustain ourselves and our children. If the birds, who are so diligent in taking care of their basic survival needs can do so without fretting, so can we!

"For I know the plans I have for you, declares the LORD, plans to prosper you and not to harm you, plans to give you hope and a future." Jeremiah 29:11

"Do not be anxious about anything, but in every situation, by prayer and petition, with thanksgiving, present your requests to God. And the peace of God, which transcends all understanding, will guard your hearts and your minds in Christ Jesus. Finally, brothers and sisters, whatever is true, whatever is noble, whatever is right, whatever is pure, whatever is lovely, whatever is admirable—if anything is excellent or praiseworthy—think about such things. Whatever you have

learned or received or heard from me, or seen in me—put it into practice. And the God of peace will be with you."

Philippians 4:6-9

"So do not fear, for I am with you; do not be dismayed, for I am your God. I will strengthen you and help you; I will uphold you with my righteous right hand."

Isaiah 41:10

"When you go to war against your enemies and see horses and chariots and an army greater than yours, do not be afraid of them, because the LORD your God, who brought you up out of Egypt, will be with you. When you are about to go into battle, the priest shall come forward and address the army. He shall say: "Hear, Israel: Today you are going into battle against your enemies. Do not be fainthearted or afraid; do not panic or be terrified by them. For the LORD your God is the one who goes with you to fight for you against your enemies to give you victory."

Deuteronomy 20:1-4

"Do not be afraid. Stand firm and you will see the deliverance the LORD will bring you today."

Exodus 14:13

"Do not be afraid of them; the LORD your God himself will fight for you."

Deuteronomy 3:22

"Have I not commanded you? Be strong and courageous. Do not be afraid; do not be discouraged, for the LORD your God will be with you wherever you go."

Joshua 1:9

"When you lie down, you will not be afraid; when you lie down, your sleep will be sweet."

Proverbs 3:24

"Do not be afraid of them, for I am with you and will rescue you," declares the LORD."

Jeremiah 1:8

"Peace I leave with you; my peace I give you. I do not give to you as the world gives. Do not let your hearts be troubled and do not be afraid."

John 14:27

Conclusion

We've seen through the previous chapters that there are many ways to approach our anxiety. I wish I could say that there is a cure, meaning that we could be free from anxiety for the rest of our lives, and although this might be the case for some people most of us learn to manage our anxiety. We learn strategies that help, that decrease the frequency and intensity our anxious thoughts and feelings, and provide us with more moments of serenity and peace. What I have attempted to do through this book is to provide some insight into the nature of anxiety, especially the inner workings of an anxiety disorder, and some strategies that have helped me and many others.

It may seem that although this book is short, there are many strategies to implement all at once. It can be overwhelming if you feel that you must do them all at once. My husband once tried to teach me to play tennis. He is an avid tennis player and I wanted to be able to enjoy the sport with him. During our first lesson, he gently shouted instructions over the net: "Bend your knees, hold the racket like this, keep your eye on the ball, hold your head like this, stay relaxed and flexible…."! As you can imagine, I tried to do all these things at once and became a very frustrated wanna-be tennis player. I realized that I couldn't do it all at once and had to focus on one skill at a time (which I communicated to my husband). As I learned to implement one skill, I was then ready to add another skill.

I encourage you to make your changes in small steps, trying one or two of the strategies I have discussed such as the "so what" attitude or refocusing. Work on that for several weeks and then evaluate if it has proven to be effective in reducing your anxiety. If so, continue to do that, and add another strategy like finding ways to have positive experiences and being grateful every moment of every day. It's helpful to keep a journal or log of the changes that you're working on and especially the results. Evaluate what works for you, and what doesn't. Ask yourself if you have given each strategy a good effort and enough time. If not, give it more time and work on it diligently.

It's my hope and prayer that this book will be helpful as you learn to manage your anxiety, that you will feel encouraged and know that it is possible to live a productive life even while managing your anxiety symptoms.

Final Homework:

Keep a log of the skills you're working on and the results:

Skill: *Challenges/difficulty*   *Results*

Please Contact Me!

I would love to hear from you with feedback! Readers' feedback is invaluable as I develop thoughts for future writing. I am also available for skype counseling appointments if needed. You may reach me at: debbiepinkston59@gmail.com.

As a dear friend often reminded me:

"There's serenity on the other side of this".

References

Cope, E.C. & Levenson, C.W. (2010). Role of zinc in the development and treatment of mood disorders. *Current Opinion Clinical Nutritional and Metabolic Care. 13* (6) 685.

Hirsh, D.R. & Homes, E.A. (2007). Mental imagery in anxiety disorders. *Psychiatry, 6,*(4) 161-165.

LaHaye, T. (1974). *How to Win Over Depression.* Grand Rapids, MI :Zondervan Press

LeDoux, J. (1996). *The emotional brain: The mysterious under-pinnings of emotional life.* New York, NY: Simon and Schuster.

Pictet, A. (2014). Looking on the bright side in social anxiety:

The potential benefit of promoting positive mental

imagery. *Frontiers in Human Neuroscience, 8,*42.

Schore, A.N. (2001). The effects of a secure attachment

relationship on right brain development, affect

regulation, and infant mental health. *Infant Mental*

Health Journal, 22, 7-66.

Singer, J. L. (2006). Imagery in Psychotherapy. Washington D.C.,

US: American Psychological Association. Doi.org/

10.1037/11366-00,01

Stopa, L., & Jenkins, A. (2007). Images of the self in social

anxiety: Effects on the retrieval of autobiographical

memories. *Journal of Behavioral Therapy Psychiatry,*

38, 459-473.

www.apsu.edu/sites/apsu.edu/files/counseling/COGNITIVE_0.pdf

www.psychology today.com

www.socialanxietyinstitute.org

www.fisherwallace.com

Support Groups

Issues I Face:

https://issuesiface.com/anxiety?gclid=CI3n057Sw9ACFYRKXgod aA8Djw

Anxiety and Depression Society of America:

www.adaa.org/supportgroups

Anxiety Social Net:

www.anxietysocialnet.com

The Tribe Wellness Community:

support.therapytribe.com/anxiety-support-group/

Pacifica:

www.thinkpacifica.com/anxiety-peer-support-groups.html

Daily Strength:

www.dailystrength.org/group/anxiety/members